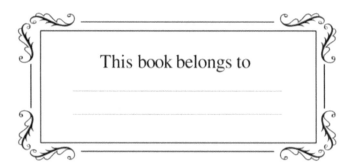

This book belongs to

DATE

TIME

LOCATION

GPS

OBSERVER

SKY CONDITIONS

CLEAR   1   2   3   4   5   MISTY

FINDER

EQUIPMENT & TOOLS

- EP
- FILTER
- MAG
- FOV

- EP
- FILTER
- MAG
- FOV

OBSERVATION NOTES

DATE

TIME

LOCATION

GPS

OBSERVER

EQUIPMENT & TOOLS

SKY CONDITIONS

CLEAR   1   2   3   4   5   MISTY

FINDER

- EP
- MAG
- FILTER
- FOV

- EP
- MAG
- FILTER
- FOV

OBSERVATION NOTES

DATE

TIME

LOCATION

GPS

OBSERVER

SKY CONDITIONS

CLEAR   1   2   3   4   5   MISTY

EQUIPMENT & TOOLS

FINDER

- EP
- MAG
- FILTER
- FOV

- EP
- MAG
- FILTER
- FOV

OBSERVATION NOTES

DATE

TIME

LOCATION

GPS

OBSERVER

SKY CONDITIONS

CLEAR 1   2   3   4   5 MISTY

EQUIPMENT & TOOLS

FINDER

• EP

• FILTER

• MAG

• FOV

• EP

• FILTER

• MAG

• FOV

OBSERVATION NOTES

DATE	
TIME	
LOCATION	
GPS	
OBSERVER	

SKY CONDITIONS

CLEAR 1 2 3 4 5 MISTY

EQUIPMENT & TOOLS

FINDER

• EP	• MAG
• FILTER	• FOV

• EP	• MAG
• FILTER	• FOV

OBSERVATION NOTES

DATE

TIME

LOCATION

GPS

OBSERVER

SKY CONDITIONS

CLEAR 1   2   3   4   5 MISTY

FINDER

EQUIPMENT & TOOLS

- EP | - MAG
- FILTER | - FOV

- EP | - MAG
- FILTER | - FOV

OBSERVATION NOTES

DATE

TIME

LOCATION

GPS

OBSERVER

SKY CONDITIONS

CLEAR 1 2 3 4 5 MISTY

FINDER

EQUIPMENT & TOOLS

- EP
- FILTER
- MAG
- FOV

- EP
- FILTER
- MAG
- FOV

OBSERVATION NOTES

DATE

TIME

LOCATION

GPS

OBSERVER

SKY CONDITIONS

CLEAR 1 2 3 4 5 MISTY

EQUIPMENT & TOOLS

FINDER

• EP	• MAG
• FILTER	• FOV

• EP	• MAG
• FILTER	• FOV

OBSERVATION NOTES

DATE

TIME

LOCATION

GPS

OBSERVER

SKY CONDITIONS

CLEAR 1 2 3 4 5 MISTY

FINDER

EQUIPMENT & TOOLS

- EP
- FILTER
- MAG
- FOV

- EP
- FILTER
- MAG
- FOV

OBSERVATION NOTES

DATE

TIME

LOCATION

GPS

OBSERVER

SKY CONDITIONS

CLEAR 1 2 3 4 5 MISTY

EQUIPMENT & TOOLS

FINDER

- EP
- FILTER
- MAG
- FOV

- EP
- FILTER
- MAG
- FOV

OBSERVATION NOTES

DATE

TIME

LOCATION

GPS

OBSERVER

SKY CONDITIONS

CLEAR 1 2 3 4 5 MISTY

FINDER

EQUIPMENT & TOOLS

- EP
- FILTER
- MAG
- FOV

- EP
- FILTER
- MAG
- FOV

OBSERVATION NOTES

📅 DATE	
🕐 TIME	
📍 LOCATION	
🧭 GPS	
🔭 OBSERVER	

SKY CONDITIONS

CLEAR 1 2 3 4 5 MISTY

FINDER

EQUIPMENT & TOOLS

• EP	• MAG
• FILTER	• FOV

• EP	• MAG
• FILTER	• FOV

OBSERVATION NOTES

DATE

TIME

LOCATION

GPS

OBSERVER

SKY CONDITIONS

CLEAR 1 2 3 4 5 MISTY

FINDER

EQUIPMENT & TOOLS

- EP
- FILTER
- MAG
- FOV

- EP
- FILTER
- MAG
- FOV

OBSERVATION NOTES

DATE

TIME

LOCATION

GPS

OBSERVER

EQUIPMENT & TOOLS

SKY CONDITIONS

CLEAR 1 2 3 4 5 MISTY

FINDER

• EP | • MAG
• FILTER | • FOV

• EP | • MAG
• FILTER | • FOV

OBSERVATION NOTES

DATE

TIME

LOCATION

GPS

OBSERVER

EQUIPMENT & TOOLS

SKY CONDITIONS

CLEAR 1   2   3   4   5 MISTY

FINDER

- EP
- FILTER
- MAG
- FOV

- EP
- FILTER
- MAG
- FOV

OBSERVATION NOTES

DATE

TIME

LOCATION

GPS

OBSERVER

SKY CONDITIONS

CLEAR 1 2 3 4 5 MISTY

EQUIPMENT & TOOLS

FINDER

• EP	• MAG
• FILTER	• FOV

• EP	• MAG
• FILTER	• FOV

OBSERVATION NOTES

| DATE |
| TIME |
| LOCATION |
| GPS |
| OBSERVER |

SKY CONDITIONS

CLEAR 1 2 3 4 5 MISTY

FINDER

EQUIPMENT & TOOLS

• EP	• MAG
• FILTER	• FOV

• EP	• MAG
• FILTER	• FOV

OBSERVATION NOTES

DATE

TIME

LOCATION

GPS

OBSERVER

SKY CONDITIONS

| CLEAR | 1 | 2 | 3 | 4 | 5 | MISTY |

EQUIPMENT & TOOLS

FINDER

• EP	• MAG
• FILTER	• FOV

• EP	• MAG
• FILTER	• FOV

OBSERVATION NOTES

📅 DATE	
🕐 TIME	
📍 LOCATION	
🧭 GPS	
🔭 OBSERVER	

EQUIPMENT & TOOLS

SKY CONDITIONS

CLEAR 1 2 3 4 5 MISTY

FINDER

- EP
- FILTER
- MAG
- FOV

- EP
- FILTER
- MAG
- FOV

OBSERVATION NOTES

📅 DATE		SKY CONDITIONS
🕐 TIME	
📍 LOCATION	
🧭 GPS	
🔭 OBSERVER	

SKY CONDITIONS

🌙 CLEAR 1 2 3 4 5 ☁️ MISTY

EQUIPMENT & TOOLS

FINDER

- EP
- FILTER
- MAG
- FOV

- EP
- FILTER
- MAG
- FOV

OBSERVATION NOTES

DATE

TIME

LOCATION

GPS

OBSERVER

SKY CONDITIONS

CLEAR 1 2 3 4 5 MISTY

EQUIPMENT & TOOLS

FINDER

- EP
- MAG
- FILTER
- FOV

- EP
- MAG
- FILTER
- FOV

OBSERVATION NOTES

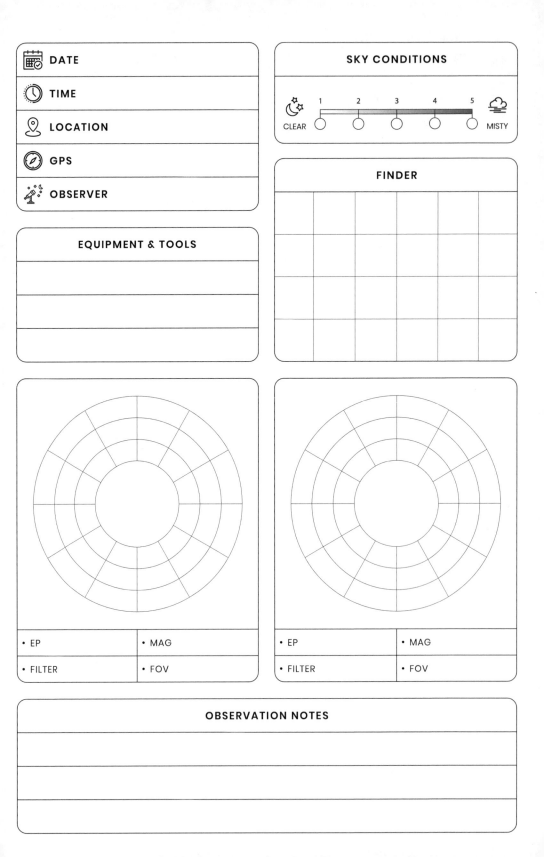

DATE

TIME

LOCATION

GPS

OBSERVER

EQUIPMENT & TOOLS

SKY CONDITIONS

CLEAR   1   2   3   4   5   MISTY

FINDER

- EP
- FILTER
- MAG
- FOV

- EP
- FILTER
- MAG
- FOV

OBSERVATION NOTES

DATE	
TIME	
LOCATION	
GPS	
OBSERVER	

SKY CONDITIONS

CLEAR 1   2   3   4   5 MISTY

EQUIPMENT & TOOLS

FINDER

• EP	• MAG
• FILTER	• FOV

• EP	• MAG
• FILTER	• FOV

OBSERVATION NOTES

DATE

TIME

LOCATION

GPS

OBSERVER

SKY CONDITIONS

CLEAR 1   2   3   4   5 MISTY

EQUIPMENT & TOOLS

FINDER

• EP	• MAG
• FILTER	• FOV

• EP	• MAG
• FILTER	• FOV

OBSERVATION NOTES

DATE

TIME

LOCATION

GPS

OBSERVER

SKY CONDITIONS

CLEAR 1 2 3 4 5 MISTY

FINDER

EQUIPMENT & TOOLS

- EP
- FILTER
- MAG
- FOV

- EP
- FILTER
- MAG
- FOV

OBSERVATION NOTES

DATE

TIME

LOCATION

GPS

OBSERVER

SKY CONDITIONS

CLEAR | 1 | 2 | 3 | 4 | 5 | MISTY

FINDER

EQUIPMENT & TOOLS

• EP	• MAG
• FILTER	• FOV

• EP	• MAG
• FILTER	• FOV

OBSERVATION NOTES

📅 **DATE**	
🕐 **TIME**	
📍 **LOCATION**	
🧭 **GPS**	
🔭 **OBSERVER**	

SKY CONDITIONS

CLEAR 🌙 1 — 2 — 3 — 4 — 5 MISTY ☁️

○ ○ ○ ○ ○

FINDER

EQUIPMENT & TOOLS

• EP	• MAG
• FILTER	• FOV

• EP	• MAG
• FILTER	• FOV

OBSERVATION NOTES

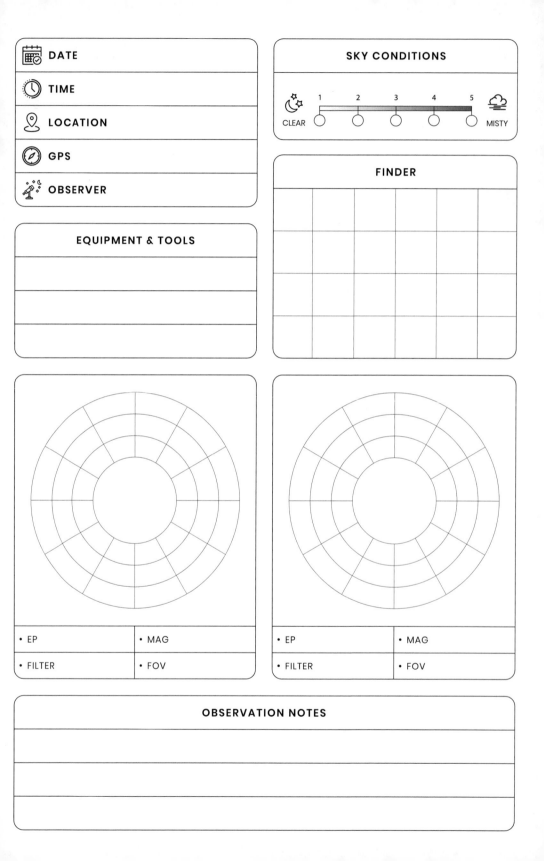

DATE

TIME

LOCATION

GPS

OBSERVER

SKY CONDITIONS

CLEAR 1 2 3 4 5 MISTY

FINDER

EQUIPMENT & TOOLS

- EP
- FILTER
- MAG
- FOV

- EP
- FILTER
- MAG
- FOV

OBSERVATION NOTES

DATE

TIME

LOCATION

GPS

OBSERVER

SKY CONDITIONS

CLEAR 1 2 3 4 5 MISTY

FINDER

EQUIPMENT & TOOLS

- EP | • MAG
- FILTER | • FOV

- EP | • MAG
- FILTER | • FOV

OBSERVATION NOTES

DATE

TIME

LOCATION

GPS

OBSERVER

EQUIPMENT & TOOLS

SKY CONDITIONS

CLEAR 1 2 3 4 5 MISTY

FINDER

- EP | • MAG
- FILTER | • FOV

- EP | • MAG
- FILTER | • FOV

OBSERVATION NOTES

DATE	
TIME	
LOCATION	
GPS	
OBSERVER	

EQUIPMENT & TOOLS

SKY CONDITIONS

CLEAR 1 2 3 4 5 MISTY

FINDER

• EP	• MAG
• FILTER	• FOV

• EP	• MAG
• FILTER	• FOV

OBSERVATION NOTES

DATE

TIME

LOCATION

GPS

OBSERVER

SKY CONDITIONS

| CLEAR | 1 | 2 | 3 | 4 | 5 | MISTY |

EQUIPMENT & TOOLS

FINDER

- EP
- MAG
- FILTER
- FOV

- EP
- MAG
- FILTER
- FOV

OBSERVATION NOTES

📅 DATE	
🕐 TIME	
📍 LOCATION	
🧭 GPS	
🔭 OBSERVER	

SKY CONDITIONS

CLEAR 1 2 3 4 5 MISTY

EQUIPMENT & TOOLS

FINDER

• EP	• MAG
• FILTER	• FOV

• EP	• MAG
• FILTER	• FOV

OBSERVATION NOTES

DATE

TIME

LOCATION

GPS

OBSERVER

SKY CONDITIONS

CLEAR 1 2 3 4 5 MISTY

FINDER

EQUIPMENT & TOOLS

- EP
- FILTER
- MAG
- FOV

- EP
- FILTER
- MAG
- FOV

OBSERVATION NOTES

	DATE
	TIME
	LOCATION
	GPS
	OBSERVER

SKY CONDITIONS

CLEAR 1   2   3   4   5 MISTY

EQUIPMENT & TOOLS

FINDER

- EP
- FILTER
- MAG
- FOV

- EP
- FILTER
- MAG
- FOV

OBSERVATION NOTES

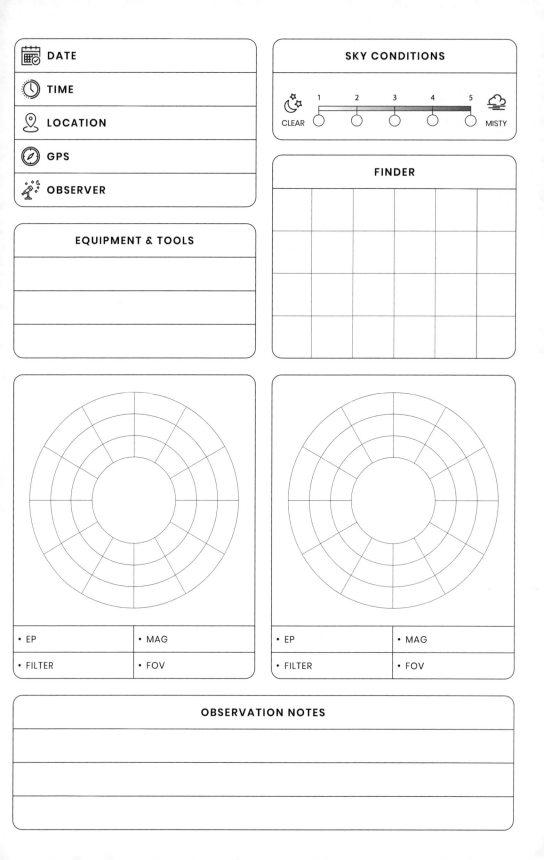

DATE

TIME

LOCATION

GPS

OBSERVER

SKY CONDITIONS

CLEAR 1 2 3 4 5 MISTY

EQUIPMENT & TOOLS

FINDER

- EP
- FILTER
- MAG
- FOV

- EP
- FILTER
- MAG
- FOV

OBSERVATION NOTES

DATE

TIME

LOCATION

GPS

OBSERVER

SKY CONDITIONS

CLEAR 1 2 3 4 5 MISTY

FINDER

EQUIPMENT & TOOLS

- EP
- FILTER
- MAG
- FOV

- EP
- FILTER
- MAG
- FOV

OBSERVATION NOTES

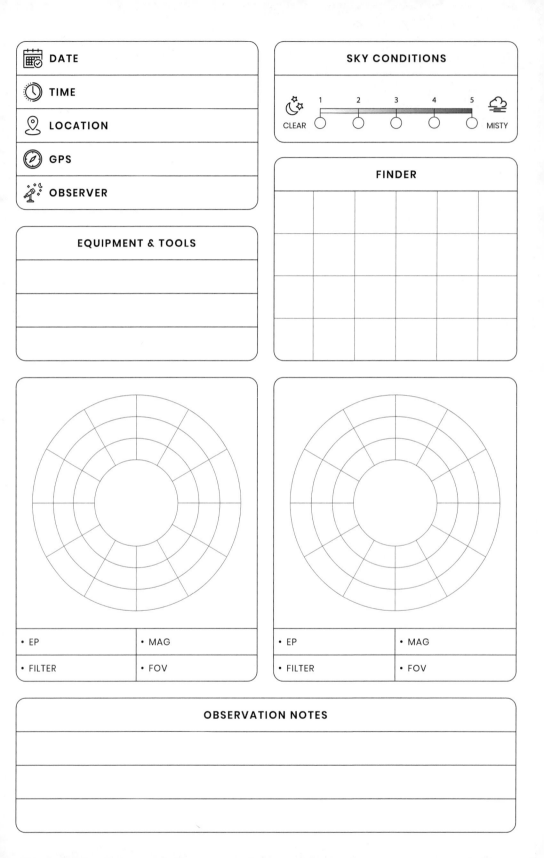

DATE

TIME

LOCATION

GPS

OBSERVER

EQUIPMENT & TOOLS

SKY CONDITIONS

CLEAR   1   2   3   4   5   MISTY

FINDER

- EP
- MAG
- FILTER
- FOV

- EP
- MAG
- FILTER
- FOV

OBSERVATION NOTES

DATE

TIME

LOCATION

GPS

OBSERVER

SKY CONDITIONS

CLEAR   1   2   3   4   5   MISTY

FINDER

EQUIPMENT & TOOLS

• EP	• MAG
• FILTER	• FOV

• EP	• MAG
• FILTER	• FOV

OBSERVATION NOTES

DATE

TIME

LOCATION

GPS

OBSERVER

SKY CONDITIONS

CLEAR   1   2   3   4   5   MISTY

EQUIPMENT & TOOLS

FINDER

- EP
- FILTER
- MAG
- FOV

- EP
- FILTER
- MAG
- FOV

OBSERVATION NOTES

📅 **DATE**	
🕐 **TIME**	
📍 **LOCATION**	
🧭 **GPS**	
🔭 **OBSERVER**	

SKY CONDITIONS

CLEAR 1   2   3   4   5 MISTY
○   ○   ○   ○   ○

EQUIPMENT & TOOLS

FINDER

- EP
- FILTER
- MAG
- FOV

- EP
- FILTER
- MAG
- FOV

OBSERVATION NOTES

📅 **DATE**	
🕐 **TIME**	
📍 **LOCATION**	
🧭 **GPS**	
🔭 **OBSERVER**	

SKY CONDITIONS

CLEAR   1   2   3   4   5   MISTY

◯   ◯   ◯   ◯   ◯

EQUIPMENT & TOOLS

FINDER

- EP
- FILTER
- MAG
- FOV

- EP
- FILTER
- MAG
- FOV

OBSERVATION NOTES

DATE

TIME

LOCATION

GPS

OBSERVER

EQUIPMENT & TOOLS

SKY CONDITIONS

CLEAR   1   2   3   4   5   MISTY

FINDER

- EP
- MAG
- FILTER
- FOV

- EP
- MAG
- FILTER
- FOV

OBSERVATION NOTES

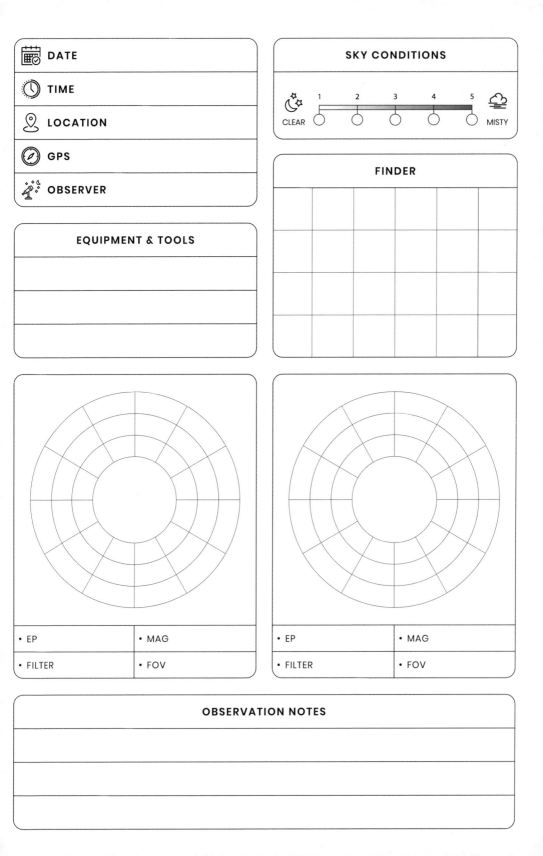

DATE

TIME

LOCATION

GPS

OBSERVER

SKY CONDITIONS

CLEAR   1   2   3   4   5   MISTY

EQUIPMENT & TOOLS

FINDER

- EP
- FILTER
- MAG
- FOV

- EP
- FILTER
- MAG
- FOV

OBSERVATION NOTES

DATE

TIME

LOCATION

GPS

OBSERVER

SKY CONDITIONS

CLEAR 1   2   3   4   5 MISTY

EQUIPMENT & TOOLS

FINDER

• EP	• MAG
• FILTER	• FOV

• EP	• MAG
• FILTER	• FOV

OBSERVATION NOTES

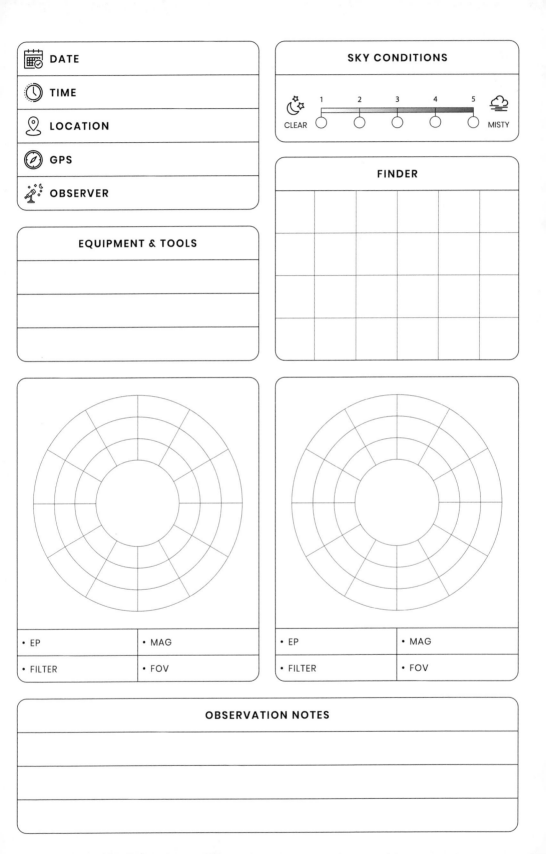

DATE

TIME

LOCATION

GPS

OBSERVER

SKY CONDITIONS

CLEAR 1 2 3 4 5 MISTY

EQUIPMENT & TOOLS

FINDER

• EP	• MAG
• FILTER	• FOV

• EP	• MAG
• FILTER	• FOV

OBSERVATION NOTES

DATE

TIME

LOCATION

GPS

OBSERVER

SKY CONDITIONS

CLEAR 1 2 3 4 5 MISTY

FINDER

EQUIPMENT & TOOLS

- EP
- FILTER
- MAG
- FOV

- EP
- FILTER
- MAG
- FOV

OBSERVATION NOTES

DATE

TIME

LOCATION

GPS

OBSERVER

SKY CONDITIONS

CLEAR | 1 | 2 | 3 | 4 | 5 | MISTY

EQUIPMENT & TOOLS

FINDER

- EP
- FILTER
- MAG
- FOV

- EP
- FILTER
- MAG
- FOV

OBSERVATION NOTES

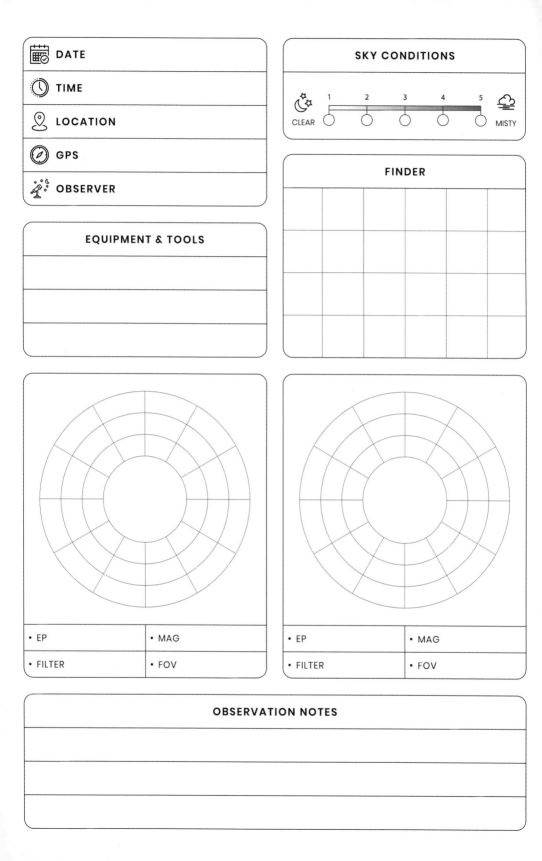

	DATE
	TIME
	LOCATION
	GPS
	OBSERVER

SKY CONDITIONS

CLEAR 1 2 3 4 5 MISTY

EQUIPMENT & TOOLS

FINDER

• EP	• MAG
• FILTER	• FOV

• EP	• MAG
• FILTER	• FOV

OBSERVATION NOTES

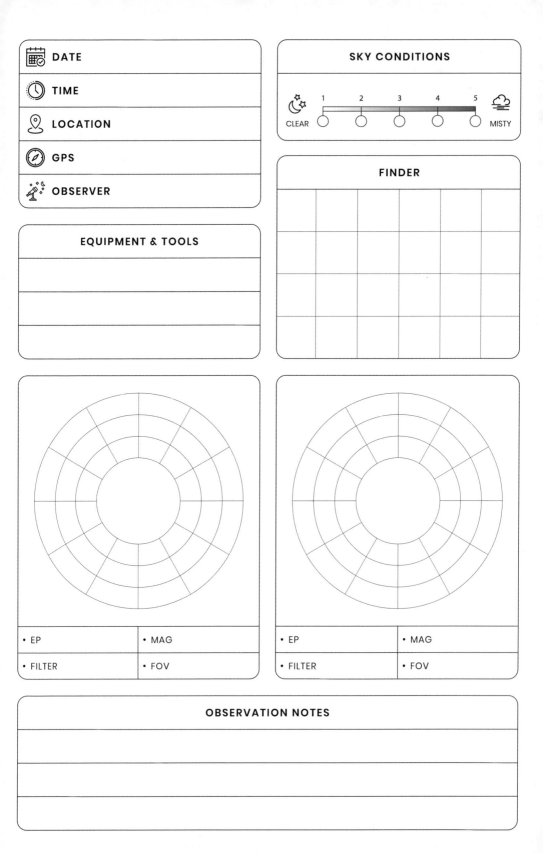

DATE	
TIME	
LOCATION	
GPS	
OBSERVER	

SKY CONDITIONS

CLEAR 1 2 3 4 5 MISTY

FINDER

EQUIPMENT & TOOLS

| • EP | • MAG |
| • FILTER | • FOV |

| • EP | • MAG |
| • FILTER | • FOV |

OBSERVATION NOTES

DATE

TIME

LOCATION

GPS

OBSERVER

SKY CONDITIONS

CLEAR 1 2 3 4 5 MISTY

FINDER

EQUIPMENT & TOOLS

- EP
- FILTER
- MAG
- FOV

- EP
- FILTER
- MAG
- FOV

OBSERVATION NOTES

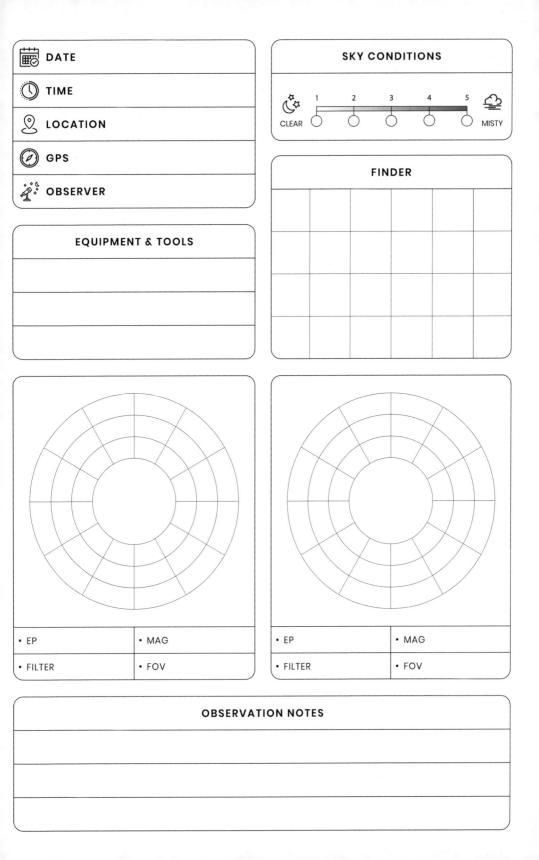

DATE

TIME

LOCATION

GPS

OBSERVER

SKY CONDITIONS

CLEAR 1 2 3 4 5 MISTY

EQUIPMENT & TOOLS

FINDER

- EP
- FILTER
- MAG
- FOV

- EP
- FILTER
- MAG
- FOV

OBSERVATION NOTES

DATE

TIME

LOCATION

GPS

OBSERVER

SKY CONDITIONS

CLEAR 1 2 3 4 5 MISTY

EQUIPMENT & TOOLS

FINDER

- EP
- FILTER
- MAG
- FOV

- EP
- FILTER
- MAG
- FOV

OBSERVATION NOTES

| 📅 **DATE** |
| 🕐 **TIME** |
| 📍 **LOCATION** |
| 🧭 **GPS** |
| 🔭 **OBSERVER** |

SKY CONDITIONS

CLEAR 1 2 3 4 5 MISTY

EQUIPMENT & TOOLS

FINDER

| • EP | • MAG |
| • FILTER | • FOV |

| • EP | • MAG |
| • FILTER | • FOV |

OBSERVATION NOTES

DATE

TIME

LOCATION

GPS

OBSERVER

SKY CONDITIONS

CLEAR   1   2   3   4   5   MISTY

EQUIPMENT & TOOLS

FINDER

- EP
- FILTER
- MAG
- FOV

- EP
- FILTER
- MAG
- FOV

OBSERVATION NOTES

DATE

TIME

LOCATION

GPS

OBSERVER

SKY CONDITIONS

CLEAR 1 2 3 4 5 MISTY

FINDER

EQUIPMENT & TOOLS

• EP	• MAG
• FILTER	• FOV

• EP	• MAG
• FILTER	• FOV

OBSERVATION NOTES

DATE

TIME

LOCATION

GPS

OBSERVER

SKY CONDITIONS

CLEAR 1 2 3 4 5 MISTY

FINDER

EQUIPMENT & TOOLS

- EP
- FILTER
- MAG
- FOV

- EP
- FILTER
- MAG
- FOV

OBSERVATION NOTES

DATE

TIME

LOCATION

GPS

OBSERVER

SKY CONDITIONS

CLEAR 1 2 3 4 5 MISTY

FINDER

EQUIPMENT & TOOLS

- EP
- FILTER
- MAG
- FOV

- EP
- FILTER
- MAG
- FOV

OBSERVATION NOTES

DATE

TIME

LOCATION

GPS

OBSERVER

SKY CONDITIONS

CLEAR 1 2 3 4 5 MISTY

FINDER

EQUIPMENT & TOOLS

• EP	• MAG
• FILTER	• FOV

• EP	• MAG
• FILTER	• FOV

OBSERVATION NOTES

DATE

TIME

LOCATION

GPS

OBSERVER

SKY CONDITIONS

CLEAR 1 2 3 4 5 MISTY

FINDER

EQUIPMENT & TOOLS

- EP
- FILTER
- MAG
- FOV

- EP
- FILTER
- MAG
- FOV

OBSERVATION NOTES

DATE

TIME

LOCATION

GPS

OBSERVER

SKY CONDITIONS

CLEAR 1 2 3 4 5 MISTY

FINDER

EQUIPMENT & TOOLS

• EP

• FILTER

• MAG

• FOV

• EP

• FILTER

• MAG

• FOV

OBSERVATION NOTES

DATE

TIME

LOCATION

GPS

OBSERVER

SKY CONDITIONS

| CLEAR | 1 | 2 | 3 | 4 | 5 | MISTY |

EQUIPMENT & TOOLS

FINDER

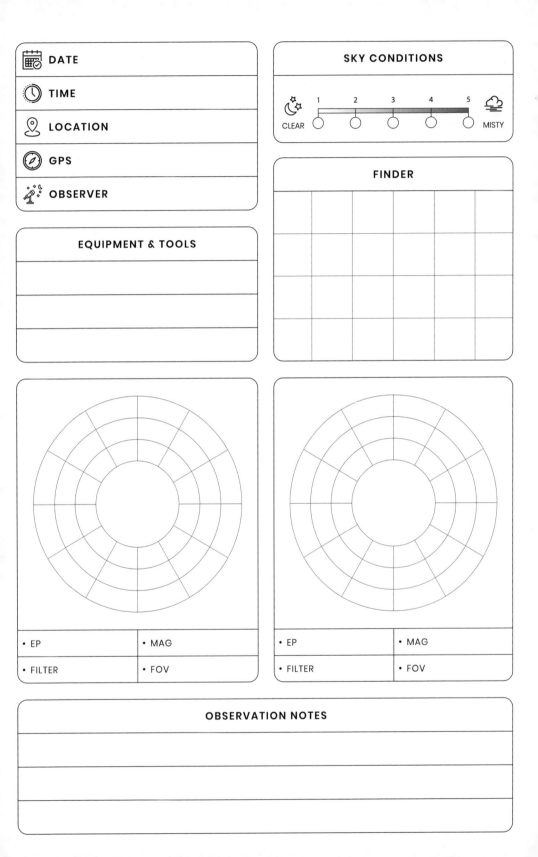

• EP	• MAG
• FILTER	• FOV

• EP	• MAG
• FILTER	• FOV

OBSERVATION NOTES

DATE

TIME

LOCATION

GPS

OBSERVER

SKY CONDITIONS

CLEAR | 1 | 2 | 3 | 4 | 5 | MISTY

FINDER

EQUIPMENT & TOOLS

- EP
- FILTER
- MAG
- FOV

- EP
- FILTER
- MAG
- FOV

OBSERVATION NOTES

DATE

TIME

LOCATION

GPS

OBSERVER

SKY CONDITIONS

CLEAR 1 2 3 4 5 MISTY

FINDER

EQUIPMENT & TOOLS

- EP
- FILTER
- MAG
- FOV

- EP
- FILTER
- MAG
- FOV

OBSERVATION NOTES

DATE

TIME

LOCATION

GPS

OBSERVER

SKY CONDITIONS

CLEAR   1   2   3   4   5   MISTY

EQUIPMENT & TOOLS

FINDER

- EP
- MAG
- FILTER
- FOV

- EP
- MAG
- FILTER
- FOV

OBSERVATION NOTES

DATE

TIME

LOCATION

GPS

OBSERVER

SKY CONDITIONS

CLEAR 1 2 3 4 5 MISTY

FINDER

EQUIPMENT & TOOLS

| • EP | • MAG |
| • FILTER | • FOV |

| • EP | • MAG |
| • FILTER | • FOV |

OBSERVATION NOTES

DATE

TIME

LOCATION

GPS

OBSERVER

SKY CONDITIONS

CLEAR 1 2 3 4 5 MISTY

FINDER

EQUIPMENT & TOOLS

- EP
- FILTER
- MAG
- FOV

- EP
- FILTER
- MAG
- FOV

OBSERVATION NOTES

DATE

TIME

LOCATION

GPS

OBSERVER

SKY CONDITIONS

CLEAR 1 2 3 4 5 MISTY

EQUIPMENT & TOOLS

FINDER

- EP
- FILTER
- MAG
- FOV

- EP
- FILTER
- MAG
- FOV

OBSERVATION NOTES

DATE

TIME

LOCATION

GPS

OBSERVER

SKY CONDITIONS

CLEAR   1   2   3   4   5   MISTY

EQUIPMENT & TOOLS

FINDER

- EP
- FILTER
- MAG
- FOV

- EP
- FILTER
- MAG
- FOV

OBSERVATION NOTES

DATE

TIME

LOCATION

GPS

OBSERVER

SKY CONDITIONS

CLEAR 1   2   3   4   5 MISTY

FINDER

EQUIPMENT & TOOLS

• EP	• MAG
• FILTER	• FOV

• EP	• MAG
• FILTER	• FOV

OBSERVATION NOTES

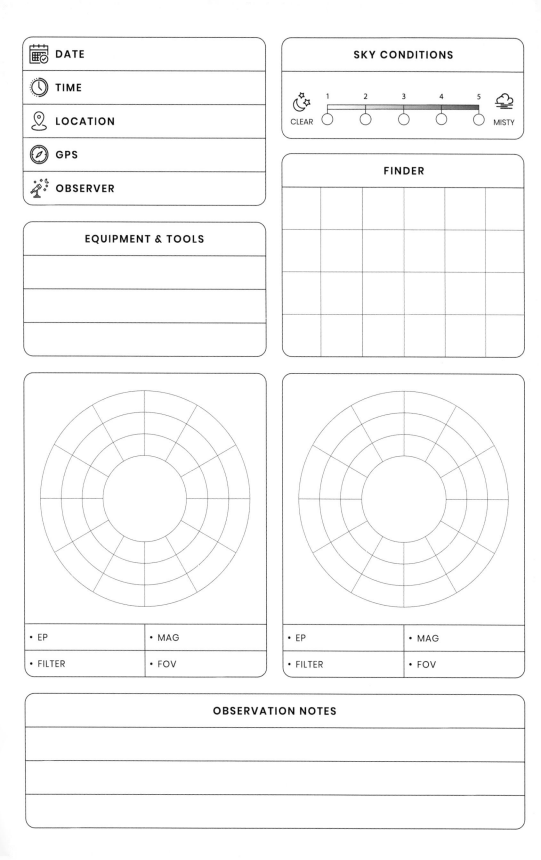

DATE

TIME

LOCATION

GPS

OBSERVER

SKY CONDITIONS

CLEAR   1   2   3   4   5   MISTY

EQUIPMENT & TOOLS

FINDER

- EP
- FILTER
- MAG
- FOV

- EP
- FILTER
- MAG
- FOV

OBSERVATION NOTES

DATE

TIME

LOCATION

GPS

OBSERVER

EQUIPMENT & TOOLS

SKY CONDITIONS

CLEAR 1 2 3 4 5 MISTY

FINDER

• EP | • MAG
• FILTER | • FOV

• EP | • MAG
• FILTER | • FOV

OBSERVATION NOTES

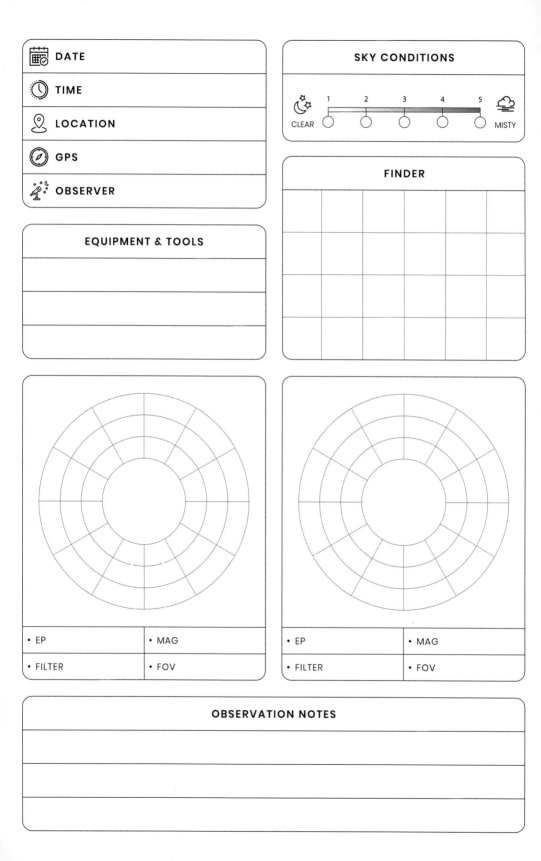

DATE

TIME

LOCATION

GPS

OBSERVER

EQUIPMENT & TOOLS

SKY CONDITIONS

CLEAR   1   2   3   4   5   MISTY

FINDER

- EP
- FILTER

- MAG
- FOV

- EP
- FILTER

- MAG
- FOV

OBSERVATION NOTES

DATE

TIME

LOCATION

GPS

OBSERVER

SKY CONDITIONS

CLEAR 1 2 3 4 5 MISTY

FINDER

EQUIPMENT & TOOLS

- EP
- FILTER
- MAG
- FOV

- EP
- FILTER
- MAG
- FOV

OBSERVATION NOTES

📅 **DATE**	**SKY CONDITIONS**
🕐 **TIME**	
📍 **LOCATION**	
🧭 **GPS**	
🔭 **OBSERVER**	

SKY CONDITIONS

🌙⭐ CLEAR 1 — 2 — 3 — 4 — 5 ☁️ MISTY

○ ○ ○ ○ ○

EQUIPMENT & TOOLS

FINDER

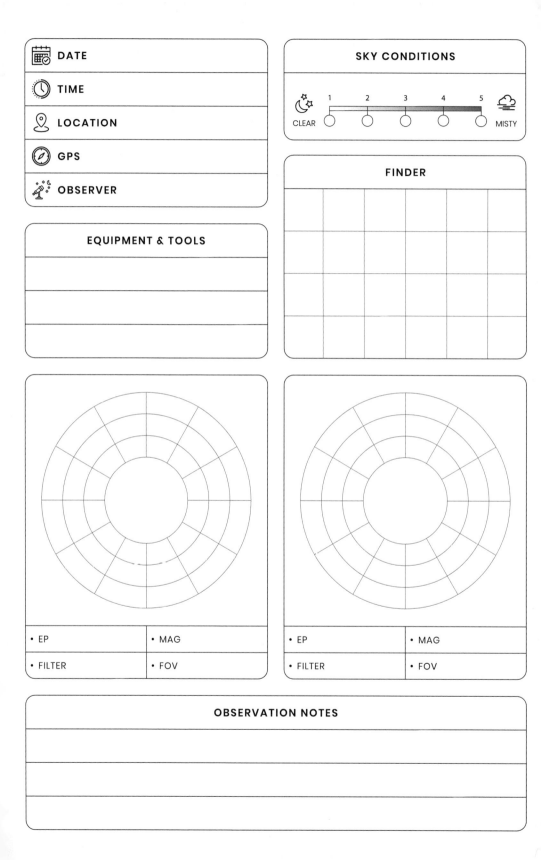

• EP	• MAG
• FILTER	• FOV

• EP	• MAG
• FILTER	• FOV

OBSERVATION NOTES

DATE

TIME

LOCATION

GPS

OBSERVER

SKY CONDITIONS

CLEAR 1 2 3 4 5 MISTY

FINDER

EQUIPMENT & TOOLS

- EP
- FILTER
- MAG
- FOV

- EP
- FILTER
- MAG
- FOV

OBSERVATION NOTES

DATE

TIME

LOCATION

GPS

OBSERVER

SKY CONDITIONS

CLEAR 1 2 3 4 5 MISTY

FINDER

EQUIPMENT & TOOLS

• EP	• MAG
• FILTER	• FOV

• EP	• MAG
• FILTER	• FOV

OBSERVATION NOTES

DATE

TIME

LOCATION

GPS

OBSERVER

SKY CONDITIONS

CLEAR 1 2 3 4 5 MISTY

FINDER

EQUIPMENT & TOOLS

- EP
- FILTER
- MAG
- FOV

- EP
- FILTER
- MAG
- FOV

OBSERVATION NOTES

DATE

TIME

LOCATION

GPS

OBSERVER

SKY CONDITIONS

CLEAR 1   2   3   4   5 MISTY

FINDER

EQUIPMENT & TOOLS

• EP	• MAG
• FILTER	• FOV

• EP	• MAG
• FILTER	• FOV

OBSERVATION NOTES

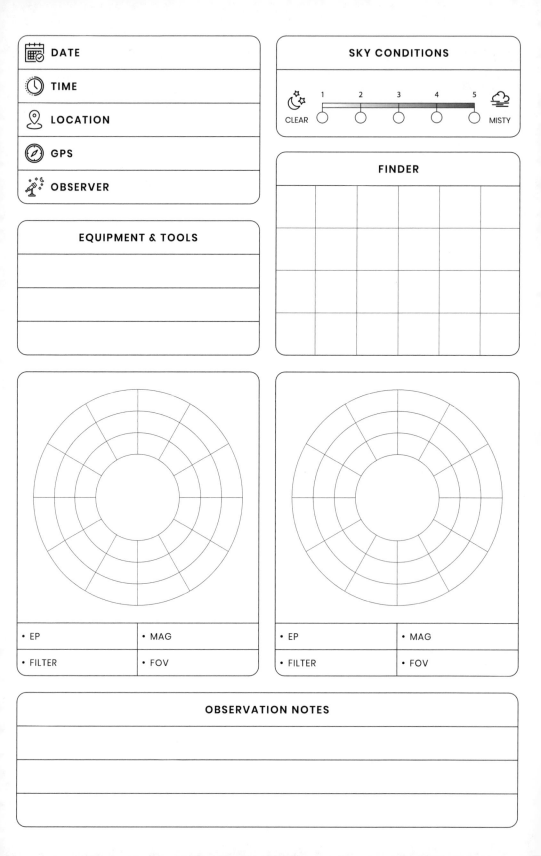

DATE

TIME

LOCATION

GPS

OBSERVER

SKY CONDITIONS

CLEAR 1 2 3 4 5 MISTY

FINDER

EQUIPMENT & TOOLS

• EP

• FILTER

• MAG

• FOV

• EP

• FILTER

• MAG

• FOV

OBSERVATION NOTES

DATE

TIME

LOCATION

GPS

OBSERVER

SKY CONDITIONS

CLEAR 1 2 3 4 5 MISTY

FINDER

EQUIPMENT & TOOLS

- EP
- FILTER
- MAG
- FOV

- EP
- FILTER
- MAG
- FOV

OBSERVATION NOTES

DATE

TIME

LOCATION

GPS

OBSERVER

SKY CONDITIONS

CLEAR   1   2   3   4   5   MISTY

EQUIPMENT & TOOLS

FINDER

• EP	• MAG
• FILTER	• FOV

• EP	• MAG
• FILTER	• FOV

OBSERVATION NOTES

DATE

TIME

LOCATION

GPS

OBSERVER

SKY CONDITIONS

| CLEAR | 1 | 2 | 3 | 4 | 5 | MISTY |

FINDER

EQUIPMENT & TOOLS

- EP
- FILTER
- MAG
- FOV

- EP
- FILTER
- MAG
- FOV

OBSERVATION NOTES

DATE

TIME

LOCATION

GPS

OBSERVER

SKY CONDITIONS

CLEAR 1 2 3 4 5 MISTY

FINDER

EQUIPMENT & TOOLS

- EP
- FILTER
- MAG
- FOV

- EP
- FILTER
- MAG
- FOV

OBSERVATION NOTES

DATE

TIME

LOCATION

GPS

OBSERVER

SKY CONDITIONS

CLEAR 1 2 3 4 5 MISTY

FINDER

EQUIPMENT & TOOLS

• EP	• MAG
• FILTER	• FOV

• EP	• MAG
• FILTER	• FOV

OBSERVATION NOTES

DATE

TIME

LOCATION

GPS

OBSERVER

SKY CONDITIONS

CLEAR 1 2 3 4 5 MISTY

EQUIPMENT & TOOLS

FINDER

• EP	• MAG
• FILTER	• FOV

• EP	• MAG
• FILTER	• FOV

OBSERVATION NOTES

DATE

TIME

LOCATION

GPS

OBSERVER

SKY CONDITIONS

CLEAR   1   2   3   4   5   MISTY

FINDER

EQUIPMENT & TOOLS

- EP
- FILTER
- MAG
- FOV

- EP
- FILTER
- MAG
- FOV

OBSERVATION NOTES

DATE

TIME

LOCATION

GPS

OBSERVER

SKY CONDITIONS

CLEAR   1   2   3   4   5   MISTY

EQUIPMENT & TOOLS

FINDER

• EP	• MAG
• FILTER	• FOV

• EP	• MAG
• FILTER	• FOV

OBSERVATION NOTES

DATE

TIME

LOCATION

GPS

OBSERVER

SKY CONDITIONS

CLEAR 1   2   3   4   5 MISTY

FINDER

EQUIPMENT & TOOLS

- EP
- FILTER
- MAG
- FOV

- EP
- FILTER
- MAG
- FOV

OBSERVATION NOTES

DATE

TIME

LOCATION

GPS

OBSERVER

SKY CONDITIONS

	1	2	3	4	5	
CLEAR	○	○	○	○	○	MISTY

FINDER

EQUIPMENT & TOOLS

- EP
- FILTER
- MAG
- FOV

- EP
- FILTER
- MAG
- FOV

OBSERVATION NOTES

DATE	
TIME	
LOCATION	
GPS	
OBSERVER	

SKY CONDITIONS

CLEAR ○ 1 ○ 2 ○ 3 ○ 4 ○ 5 MISTY

FINDER

EQUIPMENT & TOOLS

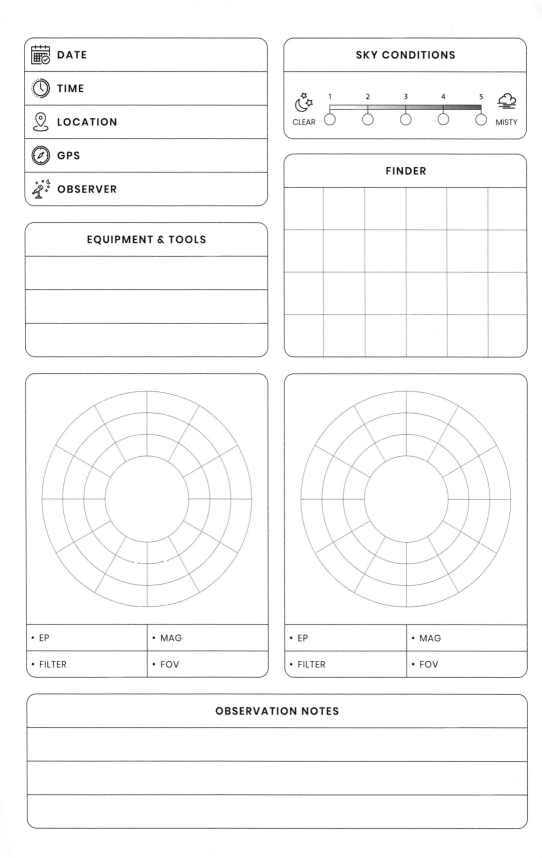

• EP	• MAG
• FILTER	• FOV

• EP	• MAG
• FILTER	• FOV

OBSERVATION NOTES

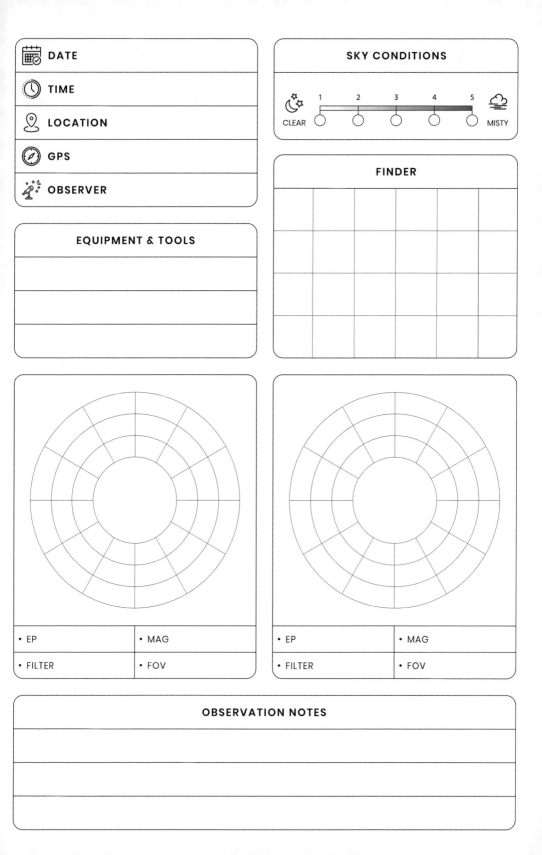

DATE
TIME
LOCATION
GPS
OBSERVER

EQUIPMENT & TOOLS

SKY CONDITIONS

CLEAR 1 2 3 4 5 MISTY

FINDER

- EP
- FILTER
- MAG
- FOV

- EP
- FILTER
- MAG
- FOV

OBSERVATION NOTES

DATE

TIME

LOCATION

GPS

OBSERVER

SKY CONDITIONS

CLEAR   1   2   3   4   5   MISTY

EQUIPMENT & TOOLS

FINDER

• EP	• MAG
• FILTER	• FOV

• EP	• MAG
• FILTER	• FOV

OBSERVATION NOTES

DATE

TIME

LOCATION

GPS

OBSERVER

SKY CONDITIONS

CLEAR 1 2 3 4 5 MISTY

EQUIPMENT & TOOLS

FINDER

- EP
- FILTER
- MAG
- FOV

- EP
- FILTER
- MAG
- FOV

OBSERVATION NOTES

DATE

TIME

LOCATION

GPS

OBSERVER

SKY CONDITIONS

CLEAR 1 2 3 4 5 MISTY

FINDER

EQUIPMENT & TOOLS

- EP
- FILTER
- MAG
- FOV

- EP
- FILTER
- MAG
- FOV

OBSERVATION NOTES

DATE

TIME

LOCATION

GPS

OBSERVER

SKY CONDITIONS

	1	2	3	4	5	
CLEAR	○	○	○	○	○	MISTY

FINDER

EQUIPMENT & TOOLS

- EP
- FILTER
- MAG
- FOV

- EP
- FILTER
- MAG
- FOV

OBSERVATION NOTES

DATE

TIME

LOCATION

GPS

OBSERVER

SKY CONDITIONS

CLEAR 1 2 3 4 5 MISTY

EQUIPMENT & TOOLS

FINDER

- EP
- MAG
- FILTER
- FOV

- EP
- MAG
- FILTER
- FOV

OBSERVATION NOTES

DATE

TIME

LOCATION

GPS

OBSERVER

EQUIPMENT & TOOLS

SKY CONDITIONS

CLEAR   1   2   3   4   5   MISTY

FINDER

• EP	• MAG
• FILTER	• FOV

• EP	• MAG
• FILTER	• FOV

OBSERVATION NOTES

Made in the USA
Thornton, CO
12/09/23 16:49:05

67640a23-d03b-4eb4-b73f-e8dcfe432037R01